NATURAL BUILDING

Schiffer Publishing Ltd

4880 Lower Valley Road, Atglen, Pennsylvania 19310

◄ The folly, mid-construction, with Yestermorrow's
Design/Build Project marker.

Schiffer Books are available at special discounts for bulk purchases for sales promotions or
premiums. Special editions, including personalized covers, corporate imprints, and excerpts
can be created in large quantities for special needs. For more information contact the publisher:

Published by Schiffer Publishing Ltd.
4880 Lower Valley Road
Atglen, PA 19310
Phone: (610) 593-1777; Fax: (610) 593-2002
E-mail: Info@schifferbooks.com

For the largest selection of fine reference books on this and related subjects, please visit our
web site at www.schifferbooks.com
We are always looking for people to write books on new and related subjects. If you have an
idea for a book please contact us at the above address.

This book may be purchased from the publisher.
Include $5.00 for shipping.
Please try your bookstore first.
You may write for a free catalog.

In Europe, Schiffer books are distributed by
Bushwood Books
6 Marksbury Ave.
Kew Gardens
Surrey TW9 4JF England
Phone: 44 (0) 20 8392-8585; Fax: 44 (0) 20 8392-9876
E-mail: info@bushwoodbooks.co.uk
Website: www.bushwoodbooks.co.uk
Free postage in the U.K., Europe; air mail at cost.

ACKNOWLEDGEMENTS

Good foundations are built by people coming together with good intent. ▲

All great projects both written and built are the result of great effort on the part of direct participants and those who help in their own anonymous ways, or that pick up the slack in working or personal relationships. So, in addition to thanking the instructors and students who were on site day-in and day-out, the editors would also like to acknowledge all the co-workers, colleagues, wives, husbands, children, and significant others who enhanced or made possible everyone's participation in this entire enterprise.

Special recognition should also be given to Buzz Ferver, Kate Stephenson and Dan Eckstein who conceptualized this program and project. Without their vision this magic project would not have happened. Special thanks also go to Heidi Benjamin for feeding the bone-weary crew and acting as über-mom to the large and mostly unwashed herd. After completing the Intensive program, student Kevin Manley threw his graphic design expertise into editing the photos, and his wonderful efforts are greatly appreciated. Danny Viescas helped the crew out with the foundation, four-square, and photo documentation of our work efforts; many thanks. And Erin Russell-Story helped with some photos, editing, and last minute drama.

The town of Warren, Vermont also deserves credit for welcoming this project and serving as a willing and supportive setting for this experiment in community construction. Last but not least, Linda Lloyd had the vision and generosity to want to fund the construction of this wonderful building.

TIMOTHY RIETH
Editor

BOB FERRIS
Editor

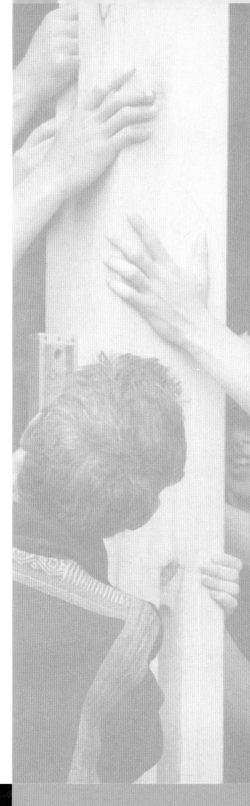

PREFACE

Schools teach classes. Always have. Always will. We wanted to do something different. We wanted to find a way for our students to experience the most usable teaching unit we could imagine. We wanted to teach a house.

Teaching a house offers up many challenges. For one, Yestermorrow has always emphasized that the learning experience trumps project progress. Our clients know from the beginning that their particular architectural element may not be complete when all of the students have partaken of their graduation dinners and dispersed. But when you teach a house, foundations must be completed so that walls can stand, and plastering exercises will not work at all if walls remain unassembled.

So we not only had to develop a new way to teach but also create a seamless staging process that insured that various educational elements were learned and nurtured, as well as completed on time. This heuristic evolution played out in true Yestermorrow fashion with all of us—instructors, students, and staff—learning and growing from the process.

We knew this was going to be tough, so to make it easier, we selected a project that was on the small side. We also picked a project—a folly—that welcomed the scale of architectural diversity and whimsy needed to give students the necessary spread of approaches and techniques. And we selected a building oeuvre—natural building—that has true relevancy in our troubled times and would also attract design/build aspirants willing to work hard, get dirty, and embrace flexibility and change.

And lastly, we picked a project that one day might be used for affordable housing in an area serviced by public transportation—all part of our effort to make a better, more sustainable world.

Bob

BOB FERRIS
Executive Director
Yestermorrow Design/Build School
Warren, Vermont | Summer 2007

Many hands...   ▼

CONTENTS

ACKNOWLEDGEMENTS.. 3

PREFACE... 5

INTRODUCTION.. 9
   About the Book 9

CHAPTER 1 In the Beginning, There Was a Model....................... 13
   Natural Building Design.. 13
   Pre-Class Preparation 14
   Enter: the Students 15
   Community Building Block: Encouragement and Enabling 18

CHAPTER 2 Laying a Good Foundation: The Boots of a Building...... 19
   Community Building Block: Food 26

CHAPTER 3 Timber Frame Skeleton 29
   Community Building Block: Music..................................... 41

CHAPTER 4 Wall Systems of Earth & Straw: A Warm Coat for the Frame 49
   Community Building Block: Invite in the Greater Community 59

CHAPTER 5 A Living Roof:The Best Hat We Could Offer 61
   Community Building Block: Guiding Ethos 69

CHAPTER 6 Clay Plasters 71
   Community Building Block: Creative Input 76

CHAPTER 7 Lime Plasters 77
   Community Building Block: Play 79

CHAPTER 8 Natural Paints and Finishes............................... 81
   Community Building Block: Flexibility 84

CHAPTER 9 Where We Walk: A Well-Grounded Floor 85
   Community Building Block: Shared Hardship and Conditions......... 86

CHAPTER 10 A Mental and Philosophical Punchlist 89
   Linda's Say 93
   Community Building Block: Recognition and Praise 94

THE FOLLY IN WINTER: An Afterword 97

ABOUT THE INSTRUCTORS AND STUDENTS........................ 100

ABOUT YESTERMORROW DESIGN/BUILD SCHOOL................. 119

ABOUT THE EDITORS 122

READING LIST... 126

◄ Stone.

INTRODUCTION

Earth, stone, wood, and straw — both old and new building materials. Some form of these elemental resources has been used to house humankind for millennia, and they remain fundamental building blocks for much of the current world population. It is only relatively recently (say, in the last 150 years) that developed nations have moved further afield to heavily processed materials for home, business, and industrial construction. In reality, the period of time in which plastics, metals, and synthetic fibers have gained prominence in the built environment is but a blip in the continuum of our history. It is also during this brief time that most construction has shifted from owner-builders to specialized experts. The burgeoning natural building movement addresses these changes with two general themes: the use of natural materials, and the empowerment of owner-builders.

In general, the growing natural building movement attempts to balance two inter-related issues, one material and one philosophical. Materially, emphasis is placed on minimally processed, locally sourced, environmentally sound, energy-efficient, healthful materials and techniques. Philosophically, this movement emphasizes smaller-scale approaches to living, and a strengthening of local community ties across social, political, economic, and ecological boundaries. Both modes of thinking encourage the use of local materials in a relatively elemental form and a minimally-processed way, which becomes increasingly more relevant in a world of rising global temperatures, rising building and transportation costs, and dwindling petroleum resources, painted across a landscape of falling real estate markets, drastically declining affordable housing options, and increasing social disconnectedness.

The economic and ecological appeal of this pallet of materials and the societal need for this mindset greatly influenced Yestermorrow Design/Build School in the creation of our Natural Building Intensive program. We brought together eight core students who worked as a team all summer with a changing cast of expert instructors to create a small structure in two and half months' time. By doing this, we were hoping to teach a small group of folks how to build in a natural way, launch a new program with societal benefits, and create a series of settings that would serve as living laboratories for innovation and the development of well-designed natural buildings. We did all of that, and at the same time, we created a tribe – a small community bonded by common labor, ambitions, and goals.

ABOUT THE BOOK

There are several sources that offer good how-to descriptions for many of the building techniques documented in this book. This book—in contrast—is not so much about generic mechanics, but is rather an illustration of a successfully built

◀ Wood.

Earth. ▼

Straw. ▼

▲ Stone and Wood.

▲ Earth and straw.

▲ A harmony of elements.

natural building complete with the necessary human tapestry. Our book takes the reader through the entire building process for the folly, and with text and photographs, documents the experiences of dozens of students and instructors as they created a small, natural gem of a building during a single summer. The processes and material result of this adventure are well-documented, but we also tried to document what is harder to transmit: the creation of a strong social bond between all of the participants – students, teachers, the owner, residents of the town, and the land itself. This intangible result—the creation of a community, or tribe—is perhaps one of the greatest benefits of such an event and program.

We built the book in the same sequence as we built the house, starting with the planning and ending with the appreciation of what we had done. Our chapters are divided as follows:

CHAPTER 1 starts at the beginning with the design charrette. Here, the instructors and core students brainstormed, discussed, and hashed out many of the details of the design.

CHAPTER 2 describes building the stone foundation. In many ways a good foundation dictates the soundness of a structure, and getting it right the first time is critical.

CHAPTER 3 documents the construction and raising of the timber frame. This wooden frame bridged the foundation stones with the roof above and formed the functional skeleton of the entire building.

CHAPTER 4 provides a description of the "fleshing out" of the building as the cob, straw bale, light-clay, wattle, and adobe block walls enclosed the timber frame.

CHAPTER 5 takes the reader to the heights of the folly as the roof is sheathed and turned into an elevated garden.

CHAPTERS 6, 7, AND 8 illustrate the finishing touches on the wall surfaces with the application of clay and lime plasters and finishes.

CHAPTER 9 describes the final building stage of the building, which takes us back to the ground underfoot with the construction of an earthen floor.

CHAPTER 10 brings us full circle and provides reflections on the building and the process that brought us there.

WHAT IS A FOLLY?

Traditionalists define follies as structures or enterprises that cost too much and, after all the investment, do not look good or function well. Follies, in this sense, are rarely self-defined. For instance, Robert Fulton probably never looked at his steamship and proudly proclaimed it "a folly." On the other hand, there is also a tradition of self-proclaimed follies—essentially, exercises in architectural experimentation—that in many cases are actually anti-follies. These are buildings that cost little and function well, but are also hugely innovative and whimsical. Our folly springs from this latter group that tends to be built from equal parts of practicality and fairy dust.

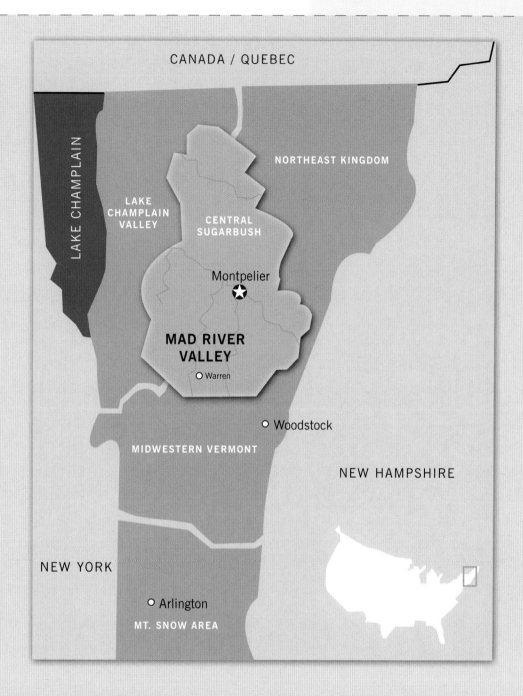

CANADA / QUEBEC

LAKE CHAMPLAIN

LAKE CHAMPLAIN VALLEY

NORTHEAST KINGDOM

CENTRAL SUGARBUSH

Montpelier

MAD RIVER VALLEY

Warren

Woodstock

NEW HAMPSHIRE

MIDWESTERN VERMONT

NEW YORK

Arlington

MT. SNOW AREA

SETTING

Creative projects tend to happen in areas that support creative thought and pursuits. The Mad River Valley may not be the seat of all creativity and innovation in the built environment, but it is rumored to have the highest density of architects in the world. Part of the Valley's allure has to do with the place itself, and what its natural beauty and challenging climate inspires, and part of it is the people who have elected to settle here and plant their roots. The migration of creative types to the Valley began in the '60s and '70s with the development of the Prickly Mountain community in East Warren, Vermont. This loose association of creative minds spawned much experimental architecture and one of the country's first co-housing units. They also launched several commercial enterprises including wood stove production, renewable energy system design, furniture, and recreational equipment manufacturers and could be considered a key catalyst to the formation of the Yestermorrow Design/Build School.

CHAPTER ONE
In the Beginning, There Was a Model
BY JACOB RACUSIN AND TIM RIETH

NATURAL BUILDING DESIGN

Design for a natural building is comparable in many respects to the well-thought-out creation of a conventional structure. Primary attention is given to the intended uses of the structure and the needs and desires of the inhabitants. At another level, governing conditions such as financial constraints, building codes and regulations, logistical issues, and, importantly, resource availability are identified and applied. Through the interaction of these multiple factors, a program guiding the rest of the design process is created for the building.

Many of the issues critical to the successful design of a structure must be addressed prior to any earth-moving and site preparation. The intended use of a building starts in the mental and emotional realm with the desires of the inhabitants. The utility of a space to fulfill a given function, its "feel," the mix of private-versus-public space, and its scale, can begin to be translated from the mental to material realms through drawings, models, and photographs, which are then evaluated and modified as needed.

Unlike some traditional and often- used approaches to building, the design of natural buildings does not occur in an environmental or social vacuum, but rather has a very specific locale in mind with its own natural and cultural ecology. Here one moves from the specific desires and needs of the designer-builder to addressing the environmental parameters of the place, for every site has particular variables of sediment, weather, plants, slope, sunlight, and other microclimatic and historical factors.

Ideally, a well-designed building enters into a graceful dance with its microclimate and the environmental forces at play on its site. This is a dance because both the building and its surroundings necessarily affect the other, hopefully not in an antagonistic manner, but rather with compatibility, ease, and fluidity. Accounting for elements such as wind, airborne moisture, ground water, sunshine, soil types, topography, fire vectors, access, and other elements that affect the structure are essential when dealing with building systems that are designed to be in a more stable relationship with these forces. The relationship is not always an ideal one, but the thrust should be towards designing with nature, not against it.

Progressing from the mental to the material and from the general to the specific, a design will move into the nuances and technicalities of building science. Much of natural building is quite intuitive because of the relatively simple building materials; however, underlying even the simplest materials of earth, fiber, and wood is a world of science describing their properties,

EMBODIED ENERGY

It takes some measure of energy to build and occupy any structure. The sum of the total energy used over the entire life cycle—from manufacture, to transport, to use, and then to disposal—of a particular material or system is known as its embodied energy. As a general rule, materials that are highly processed, shipped great distances, must be replaced frequently, and cannot be recycled tend to be high in embodied energy. In natural building, high-embodied-energy elements would likely be avoided in favor of local, low-energy options. For example, hand-split shingles from locally grown and harvested cedar are—from a natural building perspective—more favorable than using ornate roof tiles from Italy.

NATURAL BUILDING AND CLIMATE CHANGE

How we build, maintain and site our homes greatly influences their contribution to global climate change. Because natural building espouses an approach that preferentially uses materials that are processed less and travel fewer miles, they tend to contribute less greenhouse gases than their conventionally built counterparts. In addition, naturally built structures tend to be smaller, better sited to take advantage of the interplay between solar radiation and thermal mass, and occupied by folks who have the inclination to examine and minimize their carbon footprints.

abilities, interactions, and engineering. For example, moisture dynamics, thermal dynamics, structural dynamics, illumination, and ventilation are all highly relevant, if not critical, elements of the structure that must be addressed if the long-term success of the building is to be achieved. When situated in a climate as seasonally cold as that of Vermont, the dynamics at play are that much more extreme, and the detailing is that much more important.

PRE-CLASS PREPARATION

With the Yestermorrow folly, the initial layout and basic structural design was done over the course of the winter of 2007 by a collaboration of the instructors working with the client to design a functional and appealing structure that included a teachable array of building systems and approaches. The result of these initial discussions was a small "massing model," or rough representation of the building and site. This gave the instructors enough detail to design teaching sequences and course content, provide the client with a general idea of what she and the community might see in her front yard, and was a good starting point for getting the students involved in cooperatively determining the final look and content of the building.

During these discussions, the basic materials of the structure were identified to include the fundamental resources of stone, wood, earth, and fiber. For logistical reasons, the timber frame was designed and some of the timbers were prepared during other Yestermorrow courses. This allowed more time and flexibility for dealing with the interface of the timber structure with earth and straw wall systems.

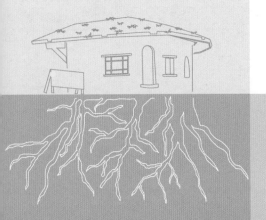

WHAT IS A CHARETTE?

The term "charrette" is French in origin and simply means "cart." In an architectural context, it is usually used to describe an intense, collaborative effort completed by designers and architects to refine and finalize a design or plan. It is believed that the usage derives from the actual cart that was sent around the studios at the École des Beaux Arts in Paris two centuries ago to collect the final work of students at the end of an exam or practicum.

ENTER: THE STUDENTS

The Natural Building Intensive Program commenced with a three-day design charrette that included the core Intensive students and most of the instructors. The students were given an existing model and timber-frame design, and were asked to begin finalizing some of its specific details. In this ambitious and productive process, the basics of ecological design were introduced, along with the lexicon of natural materials and processes. This laid the groundwork and built the common language necessary for collective evaluation of the rest of the design elements, including wall types, window and door placements, building access, thermal insulation and heating strategies, and many other details. During this design charrette, the tone was set for a full-scale immersion program that would bring volumes of information in a wide variety of topics together for the creation of one magnificent building.

NATURAL BUILDING VS. GREEN BUILDING

Many people use the terms "natural" and "green building" interchangeably, and while there are overlaps between the two disciplines, they are really quite different. Natural building as a philosophy and practice emphasizes socially, culturally, and environmentally responsible building. This is typically realized in the use of basic, elemental materials (e.g., earth, wood, stone and straw) that require little or no processing and are found on-site or locally sourced. The methods of natural building are often labor intensive, but not capital intensive.

Green building, on the other hand, looks at buildings made of energy-efficient materials that tend to have a low ecological impact over their lifecycles but could be made of highly processed materials shipped great distances. In this discipline greater emphasis is placed on improved high technologies, specialized design and labor, and monetary capital. Cob walls, timber-framing, and earthen floors are typical of natural building, and photovoltaic panels, recyclable carpet squares, and engineered lumber are examples of the green materials.

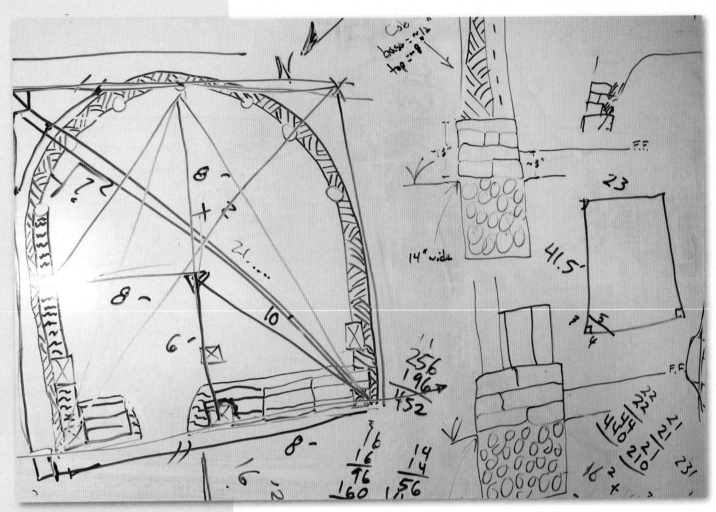

Some of the many scrawlings created during the design charrette, where students and instructors hashed out the many details of the folly.

REDUCTIONIST STUDY
STONE DANCE FOLLY BJ

The initial model for the folly, created by Buzz Ferver. Below, a second view of the folly model.

WHAT IS A MASSING MODEL?

A massing model is a coarse, three-dimensional representation of a planned structure designed to show the scale and general configuration of a building as well as that building's relationship to other natural or manmade features.

❝ I feel that these building arts are very important, if not critical, to preserve, spread, and evolve in our world's social and ecological climate. Being able to build structures that can be used for potentially hundreds of years with relatively low embodied energy seems to me to be a huge step in the right direction towards real homeland security and freedom. ❞

HOKE CAGLE

Before I came to Vermont I knew little about my ability to be creative with collaborators. I had always wanted to work and design as part of a group, but never really knew the difficulties involved. This collaboration was a humbling and gratifying experience and the reward is a beautiful building.

JOSH KOPPEN

COMMUNITY BUILDING BLOCK:
ENCOURAGEMENT & ENABLING

Most education in the creative fields is based on a culture of criticism, where students are asked to create works that are then critiqued by experts or their peers. This methodology often results in great works, but it also pushes people away from taking risks and can stifle innovation. One of the cornerstone philosophies at Yestermorrow is one of encouraging innovation and also trying first to enable, rather than criticize, student or instructor ideas. This culture of enabling has certainly led to some design eccentricities and whimsy. At the same time, it has led to some glorious designs on the landscape, and, more importantly, has nourished the creative spirit of thousands.

WALL SYSTEMS: BALANCING MASS AND INSULATION

The wall system strategy we ultimately devised for the folly attempted to balance several factors, including: the exploration of a wide range of materials; support of the developmental and educational process; security of the walls from moisture damage; integration of insulation and thermal mass, and the structure's intended functions. It could be argued that a cob wall, a low-insulative massive wall type with an R-value (measure of resistance to heat flow) of 1 per foot, is appropriate only in limited contexts as an exterior wall in a cold climate. Additionally, it could be argued that an 18"-thick straw bale wall has little place in a structure with less than 200 sq. ft. total footprint. It should therefore be noted that when evaluating the performance of the structure and selection of materials, the context for the decisions was not necessarily one of best use for thermal performance or floor plan, but rather to showcase the basic ingredients of natural building in their many forms, contrasting and highlighting their respective qualities.

ONTHEBOOKSHELF

Alexander, Christopher, Sara Ishikawa, and Murray Silverstein with Max Jacobson, Igrid Fiksdahl-King and Shlomo Angel. *A Pattern Language.* New York: Oxford University Press, 1977.

Alexander, C. *The Timeless Way of Building.* New York: Oxford University Press, 1979.

Connell, John B. *Homing Instinct.* New York, New York: Warner Books. 1993.

Kennedy, Joseph F., Michael G. Smith, and Catherine Wanek (eds). *The Art of Natural Building.* Gabriola Island, British Columbia: New Society Publishers, 2002.

CHAPTER TWO
Laying a Good Foundation—The Boots of a Building
BY BUZZ FERVER AND BOB FERRIS

All good structures are built on good foundations. This applies to buildings and social structures. In the case of the folly, building the rubble trench foundation and stone masonry stemwall served the dual purpose of creating a solid base on which to build a structure, and the first opportunity to build the foundation for a working relationship between the core students and instructors.

For this folly, we elected to use a rubble trench foundation system. With this system, the masonry stemwall sits atop a rubble-filled trench that provides superb drainage below grade. The first step was excavating the trench to a depth below frostline, which is approximately four feet below the surface. The bottom of the trench was graded to drain water away from the structure and was filled with large cobbles free of finer sediment (e.g., clean or washed gravel). The contour of the trench and the voids between the rubble

> *Stone has its own stubborn mentality about where it is going to fit and how it is going to get along with its stone neighbors in the wall. There is a dialogue that must take place between the stones and the mason, and the beautiful thing (at times) is the meditative and quiet tone of this 'conversation.'*
>
> PAGE HOUSER

Our rubble trench. ▲

Hoke and Page finishing a section of the stemwall.

fill ensure good drainage of any subsurface water, expediting its transfer out from beneath the building. By channeling water away from the structure, the possibility of frost heave—the freezing and expansion of subsurface water which differentially heaves or lifts a portion of a building—is greatly minimized, if not obviated.

Once the rubble fill was installed up to the existing grade, work was begun on the stemwall. When building earth and straw walls, particular detail must be given to construction of the stemwall. The stemwall is the portion of the foundation that extends above grade and upon which a wall system rests; it must offer sufficient elevation above the exterior grade to protect

Proper placement of a stone to match the adjacent geometry and span the full width of the stemwall.

Finishing the last section of the stemwall.

Juan José and Josh working on the slip-form threshold. Strips of masonite were bent and staked to obtain the desired curves, and "junk" stone was mixed with cement to build up the threshold.

the base of water-sensitive materials such as cob and straw bale. Long-time natural builders will often emphasize the importance of providing natural buildings with good "boots and hats." The boots, in this instance, refers to foundations, and hats to the roof element covered in Chapter 5. Stones quarried from an exposed bedrock ledge on the property were mortared with a cement-lime mixture to construct the stemwall.

The threshold, or entry, for the folly was constructed using a slip-form technique. Flexible pieces of Masonite were bent and staked into position, creating graceful curves along the interior and exterior edges. This technique makes efficient use of "junk" or otherwise difficult to use stones (e.g., ugly faces, irregular shapes). Stones and cement mortar are poured between the forms with attention paid to the edges and surfaces that will be visible. The upper surface of the threshold was inlaid with smooth water-worn pebbles and cobbles from the Mad River, flowing just feet from the folly.

Building the foundation had social benefits, as well. The stones used in the stemwall are big and heavy, and frequently required teamwork to move

The finish surface of the threshold was leveled and paved with flat, water-worn pebbles and cobbles. ▼

> " I was drawn to natural building as soon as I heard about it. I felt a passionate desire to use it in my own construction work. It feels good to know how to build your own home with natural materials taken from your own property. "
>
> JUAN JOSÉ MARTINEZ BRUN

The finishing touches on the threshold mimicking the dappled bed of a Vermont stream. ▲

and place. Care and consideration must be practiced during this period, as moving heavy rocks cooperatively means watching out for your partner's fingers, toes, and back, as well as your own. And the "Tom Sawyer" factor of rolling up ones pant cuffs and wading barefooted into a river searching for that perfectly worn cobble cannot be over-emphasized. Fun is an often under-emphasized component of successful community-building projects.

Page, Tim, Will, and Kevin stacking and ▼ pointing the stones.

INSULATING A FOUNDATION

Having highly insulative walls such as straw bale and a poorly insulated foundation can result in an uncomfortable and energy-wasting house. General masonry has an R-value (measure of resistance to heat flow) of one per seven feet, so our 18" wide folly stemwall has an inherent R-value of 0.2, which is unacceptable in a climate like Vermont's. Methods for insulating a foundation commonly involve either wrapping the exterior of the stemwall in an insulative material, placing insulation within a central cavity of the stemwall, or insulating along the interior of the stemwall.

The folly has an interior cob and masonry bench that runs along most of the walls. Between the bench and the interior face of the stemwall 4" of loose perlite was placed, providing an R-value of 10.8, thus greatly improving the thermal performance of this portion of the structure.

COMMUNITY BUILDING BLOCK:
FOOD

It is said that armies run on their stomachs, and the same is true for construction crews. In our case, this meant making sure that good, healthy, local food was readily available to instructors and students. This approach also emphasized communal eating with big tables and lots of opportunity for discussion of building techniques and the sharing of dreams and life stories. The food, conversation, and sharing were important factors in making this project a success.

ON THE BOOKSHELF

Vivian, John. *Building Stone Walls.* North Adams, Massachusetts: Storey Publishing, 1976.

Smith, M.G. "Foundations for Natural Buildings" in *The Art of Natural Building.* Joseph F. Kennedy. Gabriola Island, BC, Canada: New Society Publishers, 2002.

Tom, R., "Rubble Trench Foundations" in *The Art of Natural Building.* Joseph F. Kennedy. Gabriola Island, BC, Canada: New Society Publishers, 2002.

A finished foundation.

27

After timbers are laid out and leveled, students use a plumb bob and the guide lines on the ground to optically scribe a joint.

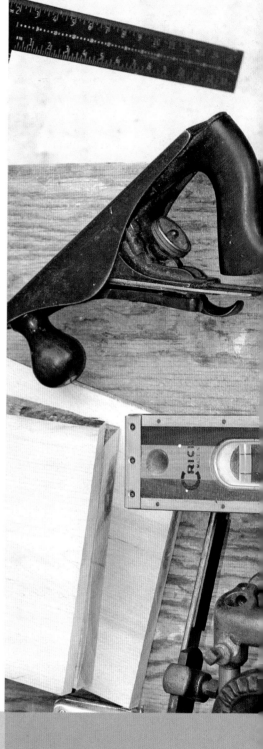

CHAPTER THREE
Timber Frame Skeleton
BY JOSH JACKSON AND BOB FERRIS

All built structures or living creatures large enough to see with the naked eye require some form of internal or external skeleton to define their shape. In the case of the folly, our skeleton was constructed of locally harvested and milled wood. We elected to assemble our "bones" in a tried and true vernacular style known as timber-framing, and to do it using two variants of the method: traditional square-rule, and scribe.

Of the two styles, the square-rule approach is the easier and involves using dimensionally sawn timbers and basic joinery to construct a frame that consists mainly of regular angles and flat surfaces. Square-rule is a straight forward, no-nonsense approach that is meant to be functional. For centuries, this method has been used to define and support the walls of everything from fine homes and castles to barns and cob cottages. The method went from mainstream to relic with the emergence of stud-based or stick-frame construction, but has been staging a noticeable comeback since the 1970s.

Full scale chalk lines are drawn onto the ground, indicating how timbers will be laid out and at what points they will join. Hoke, Juan José, and instructor Ben Graham align and level the post, beam, and knee brace above chalk guide lines using levels, shims, and a plumb bob. ▲

As an alternative to optically scribing a joint, instructor Josh Jackson demonstrates how to use bubble scribers to draw guidelines where two timbers will join.

The second variant is the scribe or scribe-rule method. With this method, round or irregular shaped timbers are used. This technique allows for a more whimsical and organic form, with each timber joint custom cut to fit another timber or an irregular surface of a foundation or site feature, such as a rock ledge or boulder. In a very real sense the scribe method invites the use of aesthetically pleasing elements, and permits them to be functional in terms of defining or enhancing space while simultaneously providing structure.

 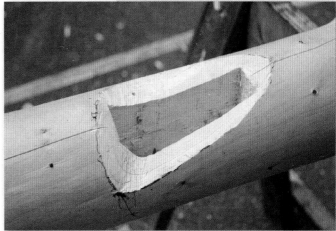

Mortise and tenon are carved into the joints to add extra surface area for timbers to lock together. ▲

As their name suggests, squared timbers have at least one square side which make ▼ designing joinery a little quicker than scribing. Hoke uses a framing square against a squared side of the timber to indicate where a mortise and joint should be cut.

After lines are scribed onto each timber, a
chisel and mallet are used to cut the joints.

32

Hoke, Kevin, and Juan José double check to make sure the post and beam and knee brace are fitting together properly. ▶

Kaylee and Will use an antique boring machine to rough out a mortise. ▲

Of all the skill sets that we encountered during the Intensive, timber-framing was the area that I was most looking forward to. Throughout the summer I collected and amassed quite a collection of vintage wood-working hand tools. Upon my return to Texas these were the first items that begged to be honed and put to use. With the joinery skills from the Intensive and my new set of tools I've taken on a number of commission carpentry jobs including a ladder and banister/rail system, a custom countertop, and furniture.

PAGE HOUSER

Before the timber frame can be raised,
marks are made on the stone stem wall
to indicate where the posts will go.

◀ Dana uses a mallet and chisel to fine tune the mortise and carve the joint.

Timber-framing is a very satisfying endeavor. It is a construction method that smells of fresh pine, spruce, and hemlock. It is a technique that can still be done mostly with non-powered hand tools and the wood is generally soft, workable, and not long cut. Timber-framing also has a rich history, and a lexicon replete with terms such as "noggin" and "dragon beams." Then there are traditions such as nailing a small tree to the roof peak once a structure is assembled, and the chance to work with tools such as drawnknives, froes, adzes, and mortising drills that have seen continuous use since our great-grandparents' time. And the fact that even the smallest timber-frame buildings seem to require a team to assemble makes any timber-frame raising a community event.

Finely cut timbers ready to be delivered to the work site.   ▼

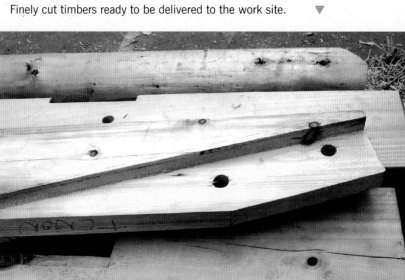

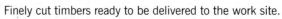

The first post is set into place atop a boulder extracted from the river across the street.

COMMUNITY BUILDING BLOCK:
MUSIC

Music is the language of human joy and, sometimes, sorrow. Many projects are enhanced by the presence of music and particularly when produced by instruments wielded by the building community. The presence of finely crafted guitars, mandolins, and banjos played by working fingers only seems to increase the creative depth of some endeavors. And late-night singing by tired people around a campfire has benefits seen and unseen.

◄ More timbers are added. Here students hoist the biggest timber, a ridge beam, into place, proving the addage that many hands make for lighter work.

Wooden rivens are driven into bored holes. These pull the timbers more tightly together. ▲

" What drew me to natural building? Look at 'em! They're beautiful! En-vironmentally responsible when designed well, and the materials themselves call for community—it naturally builds community. Anyone can really learn and do it. "

WILL McSWAIN

The round timbers are laid out and raised around the curved portion of the folly.

The completed timber-frame. ▲

ONTHEBOOKSHELF

Beemer, Will. "Introduction to Scribing I" *Timber Framing* # 76, June 2005, pp. 4-13. Becket, MA: Journal of the Timber Framers Guild.

Beemer, Will. "Introduction to Scribing II" *Timber Framing* # 77, September 2005, pp. 4-9. Becket, MA: Journal of the Timber Framers Guild.

Beemer, Will. "Introduction to Scribing III" *Timber Framing* # 78, December 2005, pp. 18-22. Becket, MA: Journal of the Timber Framers Guild.

Chambers, Robert Wood. *The Log Construction Manual: The Ultimate Guide to Building Handcrafted Log Homes.* White River Junction, VT: Deep Stream Press dist. By Chelsea Green, 2006.

47

“ *You start a-stompin' cob,
you soon realize it's the cob
a-stompin' you.* ”

PAGE HOUSER

Josh and Dana mixing a cob batch.   Juan José, Kevin, and Jason building with cob. ▶

CHAPTER FOUR
Wall Systems of Earth & Straw
BY JACOB RACUSIN AND TIM RIETH

Although only making up a portion of the overall building, more often than not the construction of the walls stands as the overall definition of the structure. One is most frequently described as living in a "straw bale," "cob," or "cordwood" house, not a "green roof," "rubble trench," or "plaster" house. Often these generic characterizations gloss the variety of wall systems and combinations potentially employed in a house. In fact, it could be argued that a well-designed natural building incorporates a variety of types of wall construction techniques in different places in the building for various effects and situations. While straw bale offers superior insulation, earthen construction offers superior mass, which can work together in concert to provide exemplary thermal performance. Wattle and lath walls excel for their quick construction and thin profile for interior dividing walls, whereas light straw-clay walls split the difference with straw bale in offering a slimmer, more flexible, insulated wall.

While each system has its own advantages and challenges, all share a similar set of needs for protection from the environment: from liquid moisture while still allowing for vapor migration through the wall (known colloquially as a "breathable" wall system, one without a vapor barrier to impede vapor transfer); a good seal from air and the host of biotic life supported by oxygen; and, potentially, fire resistance. For the most part, assuming good ecological design practices, these are largely achieved by the application of various protective plaster coatings as part of the wall system (see Chapters 6-8). It should be noted that plasters are considered integral parts of the wall system, and both the immediate function and long-term viability of most natural walls are reliant upon the inclusion of a suitable plaster base coat, regardless of the nature of the final finish (i.e. siding, finished plaster, dry wall).

Cob mixes ready to be put on the wall.   ▼

❝ Cob stompin' is a dance. ❞

WILL McSWAIN

Juan José using an old wood saw to trim a cob wall plumb. ▲

The folly incorporates five different wall systems in distinct applications throughout the structure. These systems—cob, adobe, wattle and daub, light straw-clay, and straw bale—can be viewed as part of a continuum of earth-fiber construction. The same basic materials—clay-rich sediment, sand, and fiber—can be combined in different ratios and proportions to create a diversity of wall systems ranging from dense, structural composites to more insulative in-fill systems. Admittedly, the combination of these five techniques included several challenges and compromises, particularly in relation to creating a continuously well-insulated structure. However, these

Tim demonstrating the application of the first lift of cob onto the stone foundation. ▼

KNOW YOUR DIRT

Earth architecture demands a working knowledge of sediments by designers, builders, and occupants. Most dirt that is dug up from the ground is a mixture of organic matter (i.e., humus), geological sedimentary particles, water, and gases. Humus is great for growing plants, but makes for a poor building material so it should be set aside. The sedimentary component of dirt is usually a combination of various-sized particles. Beginning with the largest particles, we have boulders, cobbles, pebbles, and gravels—all stones that have been fractured from bedrock parent material. These stones are progressively weathered by mechanical (e.g., grinding against each other) and chemical (e.g., acidic sediments) reactions creating smaller particles termed sands and silts. These particles are just very tiny boulders; geologically, structurally, and chemically identical to larger stones from the same source.

Clay is the odd constituent of this group. It is formed by millennia of chemical weathering, which leaches the primary minerals in stones producing platy-alumino-silicate molecules. The structure and molecular properties of clays cause them to swell and shrink when water is added and removed. This provides clay with its sticky, glue-like properties, the exact properties needed to act as a binder for earth building. By combining the correct proportions of sticky clay and dense, non-expanding sand or gravel, one can create durable, long-lasting earthen structures.

Using a bale needle to re-string and re-size a full-size straw bale. ▶

methods can fulfill a wide variety of aesthetic desires and functional needs while blending seamlessly in a single structure.

Cob, an earthen material made of clay-rich sediment, sand, straw, and water, was used for the semi-circular section of the building. Although typically used as a structural wall system, cob was used in this project as in-fill between the timber-frame for several reasons. The malleable and "sculptable" nature of cob allows for easy construction of curves, while the dense mass of the cob walls provide sheer strength and rigidity for the timber frame. Cob also offers a thermal "battery" that absorbs heat energy to aid in the heating and cooling of the structure.

Straw bales were stacked between the timber-frame along the straight northern wall of the folly. The bales provided a speedy rate of construction and superb insulation. Two particular challenges offered by this design were the complicated notching of certain bales to fit around the timber frame posts and braces, and ensuring a complete, water-proof seal around the exterior of the bales, posts, and cob.

A notched and re-sized straw bale ready for stacking. ▼

The convergence of straw bales, cob, and timber frame posts. The nails visible on the surface of the posts help anchor the cob to the wood surface.

◀ The notched bale enveloping a timber frame knee brace, attached to the brace with a long timberlock screw.

The Tetris bale, a one-of-a-kind creation ▼ by Dana. This small, multi-faceted bale was created from a full-size bale using notching and re-tying.

Stacking the first course of adobe blocks in the gable end. Note the lower straw bale walls and ▲ wattle lattice, all integrated with the timber frame.

> " Natural building promotes independence...it allows people a degree of economic freedom...pride in building your own place...it can be the creation of a legacy, providing confidence in yourself. "
>
> DANA DAVIS

Above the straw bale in the angled gable end of the north wall is a woven lattice of maple saplings, or wattle, framing an adobe block in-fill. To build the wattle lattice, horizontal members were tacked to the timber frame every four to six inches and thinner vertical wattle was woven between. Traditionally such a framework would be covered on the exterior and interior with a mud daub similar to a cob mix or plaster. With the folly, the exterior of the wattle was left exposed for aesthetic reasons and adobe blocks were stacked against the interior. The adobe blocks were created by packing a very straw-rich cob mixture into wooden block forms and allowing the bricks to sun-dry for several days. These straw-rich adobe blocks were stacked in a running bond using a cob mortar.

Bare wattle makes an attractive accent. ▼

OLD BUILDING, NEW BUILDING

In this age of communication at the speed of thought and rapid technological advancements, we have an increasingly short attention span and limited depth of chronological reference. As a result, we have developed a sort of cultural amnesia, forgetting that there was ever a way of eating before supermarkets, or a way of building before vinyl and plywood. Therefore, those of us who work to explore and re-introduce some of the "old ways" find it quite amusing when, upon viewing the folly in progress, a passerby will remark upon the wonder of this "new" form of building. Little do they remember that the buildings of the first permanent European settlers on this continent were made of sticks and mud—wattle and daub—not to mention the traditional shelters of the indigenous inhabitants before their arrival. In fact, the Tudor style, while now replicated with faux timbers and white cement stucco over sheathing, was originally built of solid timber-frame construction, with wall infill panels of wattle and daub or light straw-clay, and plastered, often with a lime or clay. While straw bale is the relative youngster of the natural building repertoire—use dates back to America's westward migration of the 1800s—light straw-clay walls have been used as infill systems in Europe for over 1,000 years in buildings that still exist today. Cob enjoys a one-hundred-year-old tradition in the British Isles. Across the globe and throughout time people have been creating structures of beauty and strength from found materials in the natural world.

Our challenge now, as contemporary natural builders by choice, is to rediscover the appropriate practice of working with these materials, and apply them in very modern contexts. It is this latter strategy of "integrative building", such as using an earthen plaster over gypsum wall board or putting a straw bale wall on a poured concrete foundation, that will allow us to update the process and meet shelter challenges that face today's society.

“ I was drawn to natural building because it just makes too much sense: you use materials from on-site or nearby; the design process usually involves the owner, the builder, and perhaps the community; the designs and materials have long-lasting qualities, and natural building as a philosophy and collection of techniques offers a creative adaptability to today's technologies, amenities, and materials. ”

JOSH KOPPEN

Straw-rich adobe blocks in various stages of drying. ▼

From left to right: straw bale, light straw-clay, and cob walls under construction. The temporary plywood formboard is in place for the next lift of light straw-clay.

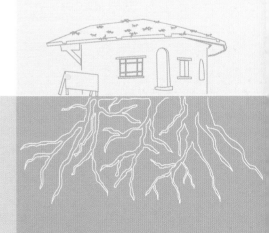

Jacob demonstrating the creation of light straw-clay using a pitchfork to toss the loose straw and clay slip.

Rounding out our panoply of wall building methods was light straw-clay. This mixture of loose straw and liquid clay slip was packed between temporary forms attached to vertical framing posts. The light straw-clay was constructed in 10" to 12" lifts, or layers, with the form boards removed after the completion of the lift. This system was used in conjunction with the straw bale and cob walls to in-fill awkward or otherwise difficult areas.

Even though the inclusion of multiple integrated wall systems added complexity to the project, this allowed students to learn both the particular working properties of each material in contrast to the next, as well as the difficulties and design opportunities that can arise when transitions are made from one material to another. If not an ideal situation for a full-scale

ONTHEBOOKSHELF

Weismann, Adam and Katy Bryce. *Building with Cob.* Foxhole, Dartington, Totnes, Devon: Green Books Ltd, 2006.

Evans, Ianto, Michael G. Smith, and Linda Smiley. *The Hand-Sculpted House.* White River Junction, Vermont: Chelsea Green, 2002.

King, Bruce. *Buildings of Earth and Straw.* Sausalito, CA: Ecological Design Press, 1996.

Khalili, Nader. *Ceramic Houses and Earth Architecture.* San Francisco: Burning Gate Press, 1990.

McHenry, Jr, Paul Graham. *Adobe and Rammed Earth Buildings.* Tucson: University of Arizona Press, 1989.

Houben, Hugo and Hubert Guillard. *Earth Construction: A Comprehensive Guide.* London: Intermediate Technology Publications, 1994.

King, Bruce. *Design of Straw Bale Buildings.* San Rafael, California: Green Building Press, 2006.

Lacinski, Paul and Michael Bergeron. *Serious Straw Bale: A Construction Guide for All Climates.* White River Junction, Vermont: Chelsea Green, 2000.

Steen, Athena, Bill Steen, and David Bainbridge (with David Eisenberg). *The Straw Bale House.* White River Junction, Vermont: Chelsea Green, 1994.

Magwood, Chris, Peter Mack, and Tina Therrien. *More Straw Bale Building: A Complete Guide to Designing and Building with Straw.* Gabriola Island, British Columbia, Canada: New Society Publishers, 2005.

residence, the folly nonetheless demonstrates the wide variety and great adaptability of a baseline of natural materials – earth, straw, wood – into a host of different wall systems, each with its own strengths to offer the building.

These natural wall systems also demonstrate many of the desirable attributes of natural building approaches. Cob, for example, is perhaps the user-friendliest building material, being very easy to work with and allowing those with limited construction skills to express creativity inexpensively and with infinite possibilities for modification and repair. It is a risk-free enterprise, and as such allows and invites free expression. These are also techniques that always allow room for one more worker, regardless of how many minutes, hours or days she or he can contribute, and guarantees a job to suit that person's abilities and level of commitment. And nearly all of these techniques facilitate our latent desires to get muddy and have fun doing something useful.

On-site design: mocking up window placements. Placement of windows for optimal views, privacy, or illumination can best be decided once the structure is under construction. ▼

COLD CLIMATE DESIGN

Building anything in northern New England that is designed to last for a long time is a challenge. In a climate in which annual temperature can swing over 130° F, daily temperature can fluctuate 60° F and beyond, and atmospheric humidity levels from 0% to 100%, with the potential for precipitation on any day of the year and only three months of expected frost-free conditions, the bar is set very high. Accordingly, there are relatively few "old" inhabited buildings, and those that remain are in various states of disrepair—or at least possess plentiful idiosyncratic characteristics—unless recently and routinely remodeled and repaired. Given this, there is a lot of pressure for natural buildings to live up to the expectations of performing better, being healthier, costing less, looking better, and lasting longer than their conventional counterparts, all while supposedly shunning the synthetic, petro-chemical, and technological-based advances made in building products over the course of the last century. Tall order!

Through the careful study of vernacular use of natural materials and vernacular design in cold climates, as well as meticulous observation of pioneer natural buildings constructed in this and similar environments over the past few decades, the detailing and design of natural buildings in cold climates has been rapidly improving. Protecting vulnerable wall systems from moisture is a guiding principle of natural building. Moisture is not only a daily threat from the sky but it is also an insidious force present in vapor form from the exterior during damp springs and falls, and from the interior during the winter when warm, humid air inside the building meets cold, dry air from outside, creating condensation. Protection from these many sources of moisture is achieved by appropriate roof overhang and foundation design, sound and airtight construction practices, effective ventilation strategies, and good building use patterns. In addition to moisture, ensuring the completion of the thermal envelope in the floor, walls, and roof is important and must be detailed into every system. In a temperate climate, every building must meet structural challenges from gale-force winds, foundations that heave from frost, and extra dead loads from snow. Appropriate material selection and application is a fundamental strategy for achieving success in all of these arenas, and as we learn the working properties and limits of earth, straw, stone, and wood in conjunction with each other, our informed decisions lead to better detailing. Through examination of the persistence and perseverance of natural buildings in cold climates, every year we are making buildings that perform better, last longer, and exist in greater harmony with the climate in which they are located.

Natural building sites and experiences are often enriched by the presence of pets and children. ▶

59

CHAPTER FIVE
A Living Roof: The Best Hat We Could Offer
BY MEAGHAN PIERCE-DELANEY AND BOB FERRIS

Roofs are the other half of the good "boots and hat" metaphor relating to natural building. Roofs enclose and protect the interior space of a building, but should also be designed to shield walls, particularly those built of earth and straw, from saturation due to precipitation. Good, wide-brimmed roofs make plasters and other finishes last longer as well as moderate the impact of solar radiation, both in terms of daylighting a structure and warming a building's thermal mass. And like all good hats, roofs should also act to reflect heat during warm periods and keep it where it is needed doing the cooler seasons.

Roofs need to perform all the functions listed above, but in natural buildings roof performance needs are even greater. "Green roofs" provide an excellent choice due to their superior water control abilities, thermal qualities, and their contribution to the site's aesthetics, vegetative diversity, and wildlife value.

Green roofs are complicated accoutrements and require examining elements from a variety of fields, including botany, horticulture, landscape architecture, architecture, and construction. Out of these areas arise questions about plants and plant zones, microclimates, solar orientation, roof pitch, appropriate watering regimes, growing media, and the depth of the green roof. All of these considerations are mixed together with the real life challenges of constructing a roof that sheds water, is not damaged by plant roots, is not washed away or degraded by rain or snow, and does not become a maintenance burden.

The first challenge of the folly roof was dealing with its fairly steep 18% pitch. Since living roofs are only recommended for pitch angles between 2% and 20%, our project was on the steep side. This required that we install physical breaks perpendicular to the roof pitch to prevent material from sliding down the roof slope.

The structure of the roof was constructed in three layers with tongue-and-groove pine ceiling boards, a layer of 2" rigid foam insulation, and an upper sheathing of 1/4" plywood. The green roof system was applied atop this structure, beginning with a self-adhesive, waterproofing membrane on top of the plywood sheathing, and an application of Decothane, a bituminous felt. Some people who build their own green roof use a synthetic rubber sheeting, EPDM, which is commonly used as a pond liner, for the membrane.

Plywood decking was placed atop the rigid ▷
foam to create a surface on which to apply
the green roof.

The 2" rigid foam insulation board is completed with a minimum amount of waste, as can be noted by the use of oddly shaped off-cuts to fill in gaps. Seams and gaps were either taped or filled with expansive spray foam to maximize the integrity of the insulative "cap."

Our next step was to install a root barrier, a material approximately ½" thick resembling felt. (A do-it-yourself alternative would be to use old carpet.) The critical thing about this layer is that it needs to prevent the roots from penetrating the waterproofing membrane and causing roof leaks to the interior.

The root barrier was then covered with a drainage layer. This material looks like a blanket of egg crates.

Scuppers, drainage breaks in the eave curbing, were placed every several feet along the edge of the roof. Here you can see the waterproof membrane (white material), root barrier (felt-like material), drainage layer (in background), and filter fabric, which will keep the planting media from falling through the scuppers. Large water-worn cobbles were placed as an edge detail.

It is meant to hold some of the soil and moisture in place, while allowing drainage and preventing mold. Drainage layers are not recommended on slopes steeper than 10%, but even on our steep roof the drainage layer will manage to hold soil and a small amount of water. Drainage layers come in many forms. There is an off-the-shelf product, like the one used on the folly, or an inorganic coursing can also work as the drainage layer. The off-the-shelf product is much lighter, but also in most cases is more expensive than a course of inorganic material such as expanded shale, crushed brick, or pea gravel.

On top of the drainage layer, we installed a filter fabric around our scuppers. The purpose of the filter fabric is to hold the growing media in place for the benefit of the plants and also to prevent finer particles and sediment from clogging the drains. We covered the bottom 2' of the perimeter with the fabric and then installed large river-worn cobbles from the Mad River on top. The stones help hold the fabric and the growing media in place.

After application of the waterproof membrane, root barrier, and drainage layer, 3" of planting media was placed across the whole roof.

We finished off our green roof layer cake with 3" of growing media. This material is different from garden soil; green roofs need mostly inorganic and lightweight media. Our mix was supplied by a manufacturer specializing in green roof media, but it is possible to make your own. The ratio of organic to inorganic soil on a green roof should to be 75-80% nonorganic to 25-20% organic material. The inorganic portion could come from materials such as polypropylene, crushed brick, or expanded clay and shale. Sources for organic material include topsoil, compost and mulch. We tried to install more media toward the top of the roof than the bottom, because some of the media will drift down before the roots take hold and secure everything in place.

Last but not least, we installed the plants, which were a variety of sedums. Sedums are fleshy plants that can tolerate a wide variety of moisture and sun conditions. They are especially useful plants if the roof is not irrigated, as they can withstand long periods with no water. We used sedum plugs which are small 1"-2" diameter plants that were installed with the roots roughly perpendicular to the surface of the growing media. This helped their roots to take hold and stabilize the roof. We also transplanted some maidenhair ferns from the site on to the roof. Some of the ferns did not survive, but the sedum took hold and slowly started spreading throughout the rest of the summer. Alternate planting strategies include pre-grown vegetation blankets, plug planting, sowing seed and cuttings, and natural colonization.

The folly sedum were planted as small plugs of 1"-2" diameter. After a year or so these plants will expand to cover the entire roof surface.

◀ Approximately two sedum plugs were planted per square foot, with transplanted maidenhair ferns from the site placed along the eaves.

COMMUNITY BUILDING BLOCK:
GUIDING ETHOS

One of the guiding principles at Yestermorrow is sustainability. It is a thread that winds through nearly everything that we teach or do. Conducting this project under the umbrella of this overarching principle was helpful because it automatically defined a common mode of conduct and behavior. The very presence of this explicit behavioral screen seemed to bring folks together and encourage a collective sensitivity as to how actions would influence the project and personal ecological footprints.

The folly stands with finished roof and unfinished walls. ▼

ONTHEBOOKSHELF

Snodgrass, Edmund C. and Lucie L. Snodgrass. *Green Roof Plants*. Portland, OR: Timber Press, 2006.

Earth Pledge and William McDonough. *Green Roofs: Ecological Design and Construction*. Atglen, PA: Schiffer Publishing, 2005.

Subtle changes in plaster texture, color, and finish were used in the interior with clay and clay-lime plasters.

CHAPTER SIX
CLAY PLASTERS
BY TIM RIETH AND KELLY CUTCHIN

Plasters are a traditional finish for most earth and straw buildings. This relatively thin surface coating or skin offers multiple functional and aesthetic benefits. Functionally, a plaster will protect a wall surface from weather, water, and erosion, preclude the creation of dust from abrasion of the underlying earth or straw wall, minimize the potential for rodents and pests nesting in the walls, and–when a light-colored plaster is applied–brighten a dark space. Aesthetically, plasters and other surface finishes can be used to add a range of colors and textures to the walls, as well as bas-relief sculpture and engraving. For straw bale or light straw-clay walls, a protective plaster is essential to preventing significant moisture penetration of the walls, which can result in rot and wall failure. Therefore a straw wall should not be considered complete until it is encased in plaster. For best results, plastering should occur after sheathing the roof to minimize damage to the wall finishes as they dry

The most common, and basic, finish is a clay-based plaster, although animal dung, gypsum, lime, and cement are often used for plastering. Clay plaster can be viewed as one of the more refined composite materials along the earth-fiber building continuum. The same ingredients as a cob or adobe mix—clay sediment, sand, and fiber—are refined through screening and processing to a finer material that can applied as a wall finish. The source materials, either purchased clay such as potter's kaolin or naturally occurring clay-sediment, the degree of processing and refinement, and the application technique, all affect the final finish of the plaster. Unlike gypsum,

Producing clean lines and details around breaks in a wall, such as the foundation stones in this heated cob bench, will create a beautiful finish. ▶

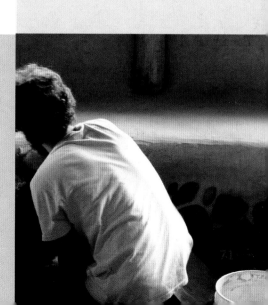

lime, and cement, a clay plaster does not chemically cure as it dries, but rather releases water through evaporation and remains a clay-sand-fiber composite. For this reason, clay plasters are not as durable as those that chemically set, but they do offer many benefits including ease of mixing and application, their "breathability" as far as moisture transfer and the regulation of interior humidity, their non-toxic nature, inexpensive cost and low embodied energy, and, importantly, they are a pleasure to work with, creating beautiful finishes.

The interior of the folly was plastered with three types of clay plasters. The straw bale and adobe walls received an initial coat of straw-clay plaster. This plaster is simply a combination of a thick clay slip and abundant chopped straw approximately 2" to 4" long. The plaster can easily be hand-applied and the large quantity of straw provides good "body" for the plaster, allowing coats up to 2" or more in thickness. This is ideal for an uneven straw bale wall surface.

LAYERS OF PLASTER

Plaster is often applied on a wall surface in multiple layers to create a desired surface texture and finish. The initial application, or coat, is referred to as a scratch coat, and it begins evening an uneven wall surface and provides the base for subsequent coats. It is referred to as a scratch coat because the surface is left rough, or is initially scored, to provide a good surface for mechanical bonding with the next coat. A middle or brown coat may be applied on top of the scratch coat, adding additional depth and further evening out the wall surface. The last coat is the finish plaster, and is typically applied in a thinner layer than the scratch or brown coats; this produces the final surface finish and texture for the wall. This three-coat system is not always necessary and some walls, such as the cob walls of the folly, may only require a single coat while others may need more than three. Protection of the wall substrate from the elements and the final wall aesthetics will dictate one's plaster strategy.

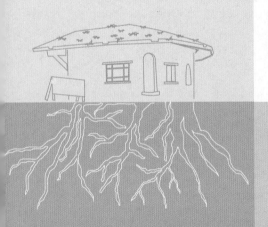

Plastering up to window edges, posts, ceiling boards, foundation stones, and inset glass bottles used as cheap stained glass offered the students plenty of experience in obtaining clean plaster landings (where and how a plaster finishes at an edge) and using plaster to tie together multiple wall elements.

75

The second type of clay plaster was applied to the light straw-clay and the cob walls, and was a finer-finish plaster using purchased powdered kaolin clay, sifted sand, and ½" long chopped straw. Wheat paste was added for greater adhesion and borax was included to inhibit mold and fungal growth because of the wheat starch.

The third interior plaster was similar to the fine plaster, but was stabilized with lime. Lime-stabilized clay plasters are more durable than non-stabilized clay plasters and for this reason it was decided to apply the lime-clay plaster to the cob bench built out of the cob walls.

COMMUNITY BUILDING BLOCK:
CREATIVE INPUT

It is part of human nature that people have a tendency to treat those things that they own better and more respectfully than those that they do not. Ownership in this context is a broad concept that includes creative ownership and the physical manifestation of ideas and visions. Those projects that purposely allow for individual expression and foster creativity as part of their design process will ultimately be richer. This is a key component of the design/build process.

CHAPTER SEVEN
LIME PLASTERS
BY JACOB RACUSIN

Lime plastering is an art and craft that has sustained relevance for thousands of years because of its versatility and durability. Lime-based finishes can be found in an endless array of applications, in locations across the globe and throughout time, from Michelangelo's frescoed (pigment paints applied to a fresh lime plaster) ceiling to a farmer's limewashed (lime putty thinned in water) milk room used for sterilization. A predecessor to cement, lime is valued not only for its strength, but for its adaptability of use in everything from masonry mortar to a thin paint or wash.

Unlike clay, which undergoes a mechanical drying process, lime undergoes a chemical change from processing to hydration, application, and curing known as the "lime cycle." In the lime cycle, limestone is quarried (calcium carbonate, $CaCO_3$) and heated in a kiln, driving off carbon dioxide (CO_2). The result is quicklime, or calcium oxide (CaO). When water is added in a process called slaking, the hydrogen and oxygen molecules from the water combine with the calcium oxide creating calcium hydroxide ($Ca(OH)_2$), or lime putty. Typically in the United States this slaked lime putty is dried and pulverized to make hydrated lime powder. Lime putty, or hydrated lime powder, can then be combined with sand and a fiber, such as straw or horse hair, and applied to a wall surface as a plaster where it reacts with the carbon dioxide from the air and returns back into calcium carbonate. Thus, the lime cycle is a complete loop and for builders: one has created a thin limestone shell over the surface of the walls.

Lime plastering enjoys a long tradition of use in many parts of the world, but is of particular relevance in cold and damp places such as the British Isles

Juan José applying the lime plaster on the cob wall, beginning at the top of the wall and detailing around the exposed rafter tails. ▼

Jason and Josh plastering the exterior of the folly. ▲

A finished batch of lime plaster. ▼

and coastal northern Europe. Its high alkalinity offers terrific mold-inhibiting properties, while its high moisture absorption capacity and high vapor permeability are ideal as part of a "breathable" wall system. Importantly, lime plasters will not easily degrade in the presence of water. This makes it a durable and long-lasting protective finish for straw, earthen, and other wall types even in areas with high amounts of wind-driven rain. Lime can be frescoed, but is more often finished with either natural white or pigmented limewash. Although lime holds a much higher amount of embodied energy than that of clay, it outshines cement not only in low embodied energy but in performance, as cement's brittle nature and low vapor permeability make it ill-suited as a plaster choice for walls in cold and wet climates.

For all of the aforementioned reasons, a lime-sand-straw plaster was selected as the final exterior finish coat for the folly. This plaster covered a lime-stabilized clay plaster scratch coat on the straw bale walls and was applied directly onto the cob. While two- and three-coat systems are often used for cob and straw bale walls, respectively, we felt that the aesthetics and performance achieved after this coat were sufficient for the needs of the structure.

COMMUNITY BUILDING BLOCK:
PLAY

From polo in the Old World to lacrosse in the New World, communities have been brought together and enriched by taking time to play. In the case of the folly team and in Yestermorrow tradition, the game of choice was the Elementary School yard game of four-square. Pick-up basketball games and Frisbee tossing also occurred, but most evenings would find some of the group batting around a red inflated ball. There is no inherent magic in four-square other than that it is game that is accessible to all genders, body morphs, and skill levels. In short, four-square is fun and inclusive.

" Tim cheats at four-square! "

WILL McSWAIN

" Will just can't handle the heat. "

TIM RIETH

The four-square bunch in action. ▼

ON THE BOOKSHELF

Holmes, Stafford and Michael Wingate. *Building with Lime: A Practical Guide.* Bourton-on-Dunsmore, Rugby, Warwickshire, United Kingdom: ITDG (Practical Action Publishing), 2002.

The exterior of the Folly was painted with a light yellow/beige limewash created with red and yellow iron oxide powders, however the window reveals (sides and edges of the windows) were left the natural lime white to reflect more light into the interior.

CHAPTER EIGHT
NATURAL PAINTS AND FINISHES
BY JACOB RACUSIN

The world of pre-industrial paints and finishes is an exciting one, incorporating ingredients from the commonplace (chalk, beeswax) to the arcane (rabbit skin glue, fine mica powder) to produce a virtually endless array of finishes, from semi-transparent washes and glosses to full-opacity glossy paints. While not every material is inherently non-toxic, many of the paints and finishes made from natural ingredients are not only healthier for the inhabitant than conventional synthetic paints, but relatively benign for the applier, as well.

One of the most enticing aspects of working with natural paints and finishes comes from the freedom and creativity enjoyed in their creation. Making one's own paints requires equal parts chemist, builder, artist, and craftsperson. Working with paints of one's own creation can be at times challenging, at times delightfully simple, and almost always tremendously rewarding. The process moves through the various creative processes of: achieving desired colors by mixing clay and mineral pigments; adjusting the mix for appropriate opacity; perfecting the consistency for smooth and adhesive application to the wall substrate; ensuring the durability and integrity, both during the curing/drying process and for the long-term presence in the room.

With the folly, we continued our study of lime by preparing and applying a traditional limewash as a protective layer over the exterior plaster. Two coats of un-pigmented limewash and a final pigmented coat were applied. The limewash atop the exterior lime plaster was an appropriate finish that helped the folly nestle into its woodland location by softening the striking white natural lime color with a gentler beige pigment.

COMMUNITY BUILDING BLOCK:
FLEXIBILITY

Projects that are rigid and doctrinaire do not lend themselves to community building. "My way or the highway" approaches forced into the realm of collective actions may lead to some temporary level of efficiency, but also tend to drive good people away. Purposely leave some wiggle room in projects, and then, use it.

Flexibility is an important attribute in natural building... ▲

... but there is such a thing as being *too* relaxed. ▲

ONTHEBOOKSHELF

Lawless, Julia and Lynn Edwards. *The Natural Paint Book*. New York: Rodale Press, 2003.

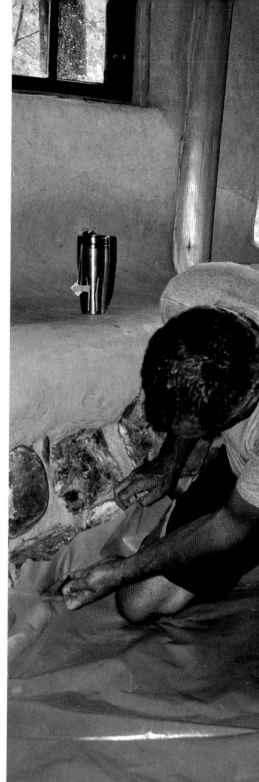

Page placing the plastic sheeting atop the subfloor. This plastic sheet will act as a water barrier, preventing the capillary movement of ground water up into the earthen floor material. ▶

CHAPTER NINE
WHERE WE WALK: A WELL-GROUNDED FLOOR
BY TIM RIETH

Earth is the oldest flooring system, and is still common in many parts of the world today. Packed and compressed, perhaps sealed with oil, dung, or animal blood, an earthen floor can be a durable and aesthetically pleasing surface. This floor finish is enjoying renewed popularity in developed countries where it can be incorporated into existing structures or newly constructed buildings, be they natural, green, or conventional in design and materials.

Designing and building an earthen floor in a challenging climate such as Vermont requires particular care in relation to water/moisture and thermal properties. The abundance of surface and subsurface water in Vermont and the extreme cold, combined with minimal sunlight during winter months, requires specific detailing of the floor. The design and construction of the folly floor provides one example to address these issues.

Two-inch rigid foam boards were used for insulation. Each board was scribed to meet the ▼
irregular face of the stone foundation and all of the seams were sealed with duct tape.

Almost everyone in the Intensive group was in some sort of transition. We embraced one another for our individuality, levels of skill, love of life and its constantly changing and challenging situations. We saw our collective as a whole instead of the disparate parts, and we are a group of like-minded souls.

PAGE HOUSER

85

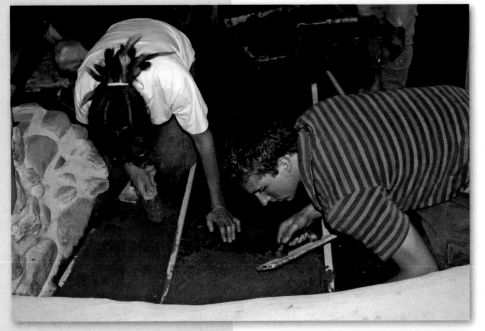

COMMUNITY BUILDING BLOCK:
SHARED HARDSHIP AND CONDITIONS

Sharing across the board is a good practice in community projects. Over the course of this project we were able to observe that campers bonded more closely with other campers than they did with those who elected to spend the summer under a roof. This was also evident with core versus non-core students who did not take the entire series of classes. Time and conditions tended to form circles of incremental intimacy, with long-term campers at the center and the single-class bed-and-breakfasters at the outer rim.

◁ Students used ½" thick lumber as guides and troweled-on the final floor surface using a wooden pool float to compact and work the clay-sand-straw mix into place. Then, a steel trowel was used to create a "floated" surface. "Floating" the surface pushes the coarser sand particles into the mix while pulling a thin layer of clay-rich water to the surface, creating a smooth finish.

ON THE BOOKSHELF

Steen, Athena and Bill Steen. *Earthen Floors.* Elgin, AZ, Canelo Project, 1996.

Steen, Athena and Bill Steen. "Earthen Floors" in *The Art of Natural Building.* Joseph F. Kennedy, Michael G. Smith, and Catherine Wanek (eds). Gabriola Island, British Columbia: New Society Publishers, 2002.

Evans, Ianto, Michael G. Smith, and Linda Smiley. *The Hand-Sculpted House.* White River Junction, Vermont: Chelsea Green, 2002.

◁ Atop the rigid foam, lifts of "road base" were tamped into place in 1.5" lifts.

The folly floor is approximately 120 ft^2 and consists of seven inches of material, which can be divided into four distinct layers. First, a plastic sheet was placed above a well-tamped and leveled subfloor of sediment to create a moisture barrier. Second, 2" rigid foam boards were installed and the seams were sealed with tape to insulate the floor. Third, 4.5" of "road base"---a mixture of gravel, pebbles, sand, silt, and a small proportion of clay---were tamped into place in 1.5" lifts. The final surface of this third layer was diligently compacted and leveled, in preparation for the finish floor layer. The fourth and finish floor layer, which consisted of a 1:5 ratio of clay slip and sifted sand with a small proportion of finely milled straw, was applied as a uniform 1/2" layer. The layer was trowelled onto the even road base surface using wooden trowels to initially compact the material and finally "floated" with steel trowels to create a smoother surface. Powdered iron oxide pigment was applied to this floated surface and passed over with a steel trowel to produce a streaked "comet-tail" affect. Last, multiple coats of linseed oil were applied and a final coat of melted bee's wax and linseed oil was burnished onto the surface.

Josh paying particular attention to the edge detail where the finish floor meets the stone threshold. ▲

A dry, iron-oxide pigment was sprinkled onto the floated floor surface and trowelled into place, creating a streaked finish. ▼

CHAPTER TEN
A MENTAL AND PHILOSOPHICAL PUNCHLIST
BY TIM RIETH AND BOB FERRIS

Perhaps working with earth, straw, stone, and wood appears to be a circuitous route to developing community, and perhaps not. The socio-cultural, ecological, and economic benefits of natural building are apparent, but when parsed down, this method and philosophy of building is also a vehicle for community building. In a culture that measures things by cost in dollars and cents, we can pay for expensive buildings constructed with hired labor, or we can opt for labor-intensive, owner-built houses. This apparent challenge is really a boon; a boon for developing the relationships that are so often lacking in our 21st century lives, the relationships that we pine for as we discuss rural cultures, sentimentalize about colonial America, or just have a nagging feeling that something is not right with lives lived in purposely isolated homes, cars, and offices. *Homo sapiens* are social creatures, and these hard-wired social needs are not adequately satisfied by television, email, and iPods, as much as we fill our time with such luxuries. Social needs are filled by the blood, sweat, tears, and laughter that can be found when two or more people get together to mix cob, stack bales, scribe timbers, and lay stone.

Graduation day. ▼

The crew: (left to right) Linda Lloyd, program host/client, Buzz Ferver, instructor, Kevin Manley, Page Houser, Tim Rieth, Will McSwain, Dana Davis, Jacob Racusin and Mimi (in front), Josh Koppen, Juan José Martinez Brun, Jason Price, Hoke Cagle.

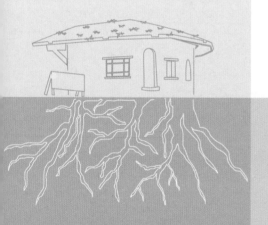

It is a truism that many hands make for a lighter load, but this does not relate solely to the increased speed of finishing a task. Rather, the enjoyment that can be found in such collaborative work makes the work itself seem, well, fun. In fact, the association of the word "work"—a word laden with negative connotations in our culture—with enjoyment is often foreign for many of us. But this is the reality for so many venturing down this path. We have outlined here one experiment, if you will, that brings together all of these materials; an experiment in education; an experiment in using earth, straw, stone, and wood to take many individuals and form a cohesive group – indeed, a community.

People and posts are both needed for support. ▲

This was a great process to watch. These folks came here from a dozen or so states and two countries, yet three weeks into the program, in the morning we would find many of them marching down the hill from their campsites in single file, à la 'Hi-ho, hi-ho, it's off to work we go'....It was a joy to watch the progression.

BOB FERRIS

LINDA LLOYD
PROGRAM HOST & CLIENT

Linda Lloyd served on the Yestermorrow Board of Directors for nine years, and is currently the Executive Director of the Mad River Valley Planning District.

LINDA'S SAY

❝ For me, the folly project was a way to complete a natural building in a very visible place in Warren Village. The covered bridge below the folly site has many daily visitors who were treated to a view of the students' and instructors' labors as the building took shape. Concurrently, my home was being built on the same property. This property had formerly been the residence for a falling-to-pieces mobile home and thirty tons of debris that I had removed, so there was already a lot of interest in what was happening on the site. People would ask me, on a regular basis,, "What is that mud hut?," or "What's happening on your property?" To these comments I always suggested that people should stop by for a visit, and the folks that did were treated to a tour by the students and learned about the structure and the group that was building it. Some even asked about using the folly for small meetings since it had such a wonderful feeling.

Although I had thought the building was about exposing people to natural building, I found that it was about much more; it was about the incredible energy and thought and craftsmanship put into it by the students. It was about me letting go of some of my personal design choices and realizing that the folly was "their" structure. It was about a group of students there until almost 11:00 PM one night trying to work out the kinks in the rocket stove, and succeeding. It was about the students bringing their visiting parents or significant others to see what they had created.

As I said at the students' graduation ceremony, "This is your folly and please feel free to come and visit it anytime." The folly is intended to have an addition built next year, which may include a bath, kitchenette and loft bedroom. That structure will now need to be totally redesigned so that it fits in with the quality and character of the folly and honors the original builders. Imagine how wonderful it would be when they come back for a Yestermorrow class, to actually stay in this wonderful, natural building. ❞

Linda Lloyd ▲

93

The folly has become something of a tourist attraction in Warren. ▶

COMMUNITY BUILDING BLOCK:
RECOGNITION AND PRAISE

People shine in the light of praise. But it is often ignored, misapplied, or used so casually as to be meaningless. With a community-building project, praise and recognition are great motivators and should be judiciously and generously employed. Throughout this project, folks were praised for accomplishments and contributions in an even-handed manner and in a scale suitable for the accomplishment. At the end of the project all core students were recognized individually for their contributions. This was orchestrated in a manner and detail that indicated that someone had taken the time to watch what they were doing and recognize their achievements and growth within the context of the program and within the greater community of which they were now full members.

THE FOLLY IN WINTER
AN AFTERWORD

Winter's snows bring reflection. The soft blanket of flakes seems to dampen sound and slow time. Peace settles on the landscape and in the mind. And once the calm sets in, we, in the whiteness, think. We think about summer's brilliance and the 4th of July parade. We think about new ways to bring light, laughter, and exercise into our lives as the mercury and our daily ration of natural lumens drops, and then drops lower. And we make ready for next year.

For the Natural Building Intensive, this means looking at what worked and did not work. We then begin the process of incorporating those lessons into the next set of classes and projects. We also reflect on having had an impact on people's lives. For instance, Josh Koppen is still here on campus and in 2008 will be our Kitchen and Garden Intern. Juan José Martinez Brun left Guadalajara and moved his family to Moretown in the northern end of the Mad River Valley—quite a change for a person whose idea of footwear tends towards flip-flops, and who often wore a serape vest to fend off the chill of our mild summers. Dana Davis was also caught by the Valley magnet, bought land not far from the folly, and hopes to build there.

Not all was good. We are still wrestling some with the green roof and are looking to fine-tune its design and execution. Former intern Christian Peterson, known to all as the "Cob Cowboy," cut his foot seriously on a piece of glass while cob-stomping, and had to be stitched and re-stitched. We also found that it was difficult to inject transient students into the core student and teacher mix; these educational stepchildren got the techniques, but not the full social benefit. The students wanted more work on and exposure to the infrastructural elements of a home that keeps us warm, and helps us both prepare food and have light when the sun goes down. And we also stumbled a few times as hosts in breaking the code for accommodating students who actually lived here lock, stock, and barrel for months, versus those who were only visiting for a week or a weekend.

(cont'd.)

97

◀ On the threshold of winter.

Snow caps the green roof while sun soaks the walls on a frigid winter day. ▶

And so the design cycle begins again and we populate the charrette flip charts with questions. How do we modify the green roof design to be more natural and work better for all concerned? How do we make certain that none of the instructors or students spend time in the local emergency room in a world of bare feet? Do we want to attempt a project that incorporates heating, cooking, and electrical systems? And what campus changes, beyond dedicated student mailboxes, are required to make life easier for those who migrate temporarily to our Valley?

Life goes on, and in the spring we will be watching grain shoots that will grow and ultimately become straw bales. We will also be canvassing local foresters on raw log supplies for the timber-frames and scouting for sand, rock, and clay resources. Ideas and dreams will be translated into rough drawings, which will transmute into models. And by September we will see another structure grow out of the process that we call design/build.

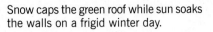

BOB FERRIS
Winter 2007

ABOUT
THE INSTRUCTORS

ANDY BURT
NATURAL BUILDING DESIGN CHARRETTE, BUILDING FOUNDATIONS, CLAY PLASTER

Andy is a hearty young fellow who has a fervent passion for building with natural materials. After a stint with the Cob Cottage Company, Andy has been teaching workshops and experimenting with clay, sand, and straw. He currently shares life with his partner and two boys on a homestead in Oregon.

KELLY CUTCHIN
CLAY PLASTERS, NATURAL PAINTS AND FINISHES

Kelly has a B.A. in Sustainability and Environmental Studies from Berea College. Following graduation, she spent a year on a Thomas J. Watson Fellowship traveling to Turkey, Italy, Tunisia, South Africa, Swaziland, Lesotho and Japan studying traditional building methods and their potential application in modern ecological design. After interning at Yestermorrow, she spent half a year making fine wooden furniture in coastal New England and has been busy building and plastering ecologically designed homes in the area ever since.

ALLAN "BUZZ" FERVER
NATURAL BUILDING DESIGN CHARRETTE, BUILDING FOUNDATIONS, ROCKET STOVE, GREEN
ROOF DESIGN AND INSTALLATION

Buzz was trained in Ornamental Horticulture and Landscape Design in
the 1970s. He switched careers to work as an independent building
designer and contractor in 1980. Parallel careers as a product design
engineer for an automotive tool and equipment manufacturer, and mar-
keting and sales agent for a huge processor of compost made his life
even more interesting. The 21st century finds him back as a Design/
Builder, focusing primarily on new homes and major renovations to
existing homes as a partner in Overbrook Design. He still spends some
time consulting for the compost industry, and dabbles in Sustainable
Agriculture. A stormwater-head, for fun he follows the implications of
the Clean Water Act and the ever-evolving NPDES Phase II rules. He
is currently living in and building a solar home in Worcester, Vermont
with his beautiful wife Sandra. He has been teaching since 1970.

BEN GRAHAM
NATURAL BUILDING DESIGN CHARRETTE, TIMBER FRAMING OUTSIDE THE BOX – SCRIBE METHODS

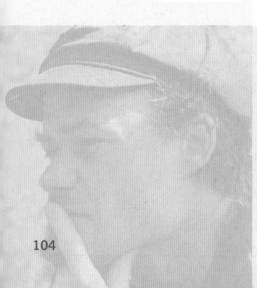

While studying architecture at the Rhode Island School of Design, Ben traveled West and East learning about building that was more consciously and respectfully connected with its surrounding ecology and culture. Settling in the central Green Mountains of Vermont he has set up a design/build company trying out combinations of new and old techniques in hopes of spurring more interest in low-impact construction. Ben has lived in, studied and organized intentional community developments. This work, along with ecological design as well as some puppet-making, has been the foundation for his most visionary work in planning for sustainable communities. He co-founded the non-profit organization SpiralWorks (www.naturaldesignbuild.us) to address these issues. He also serves on the Plainfield Planning Commission in Central Vermont.

JOSH JACKSON
TIMBER FRAMING OUTSIDE THE BOX – SCRIBE METHODS

Josh has a B.S.M.E. from Yale. He fell in love with timber-framing and ecological building at the Heartwood School and has pursued these paths through a wide variety of natural materials, handmade paper, stained glass, and of course timbers of all shapes, sizes, and species. He delights in the creation of homes that nourish community during the building process, and that provide healthy, soulful, beautiful shelter. Josh recently co-founded Humble Abode Design/Build (www.humbleabode.biz) to continue this work.

MEAGHAN PIERCE-DELANEY
NATURAL BUILDING DESIGN CHARRETTE, GREEN ROOF DESIGN AND INSTALLATION

Meaghan graduated from University of Pennsylvania in May 2006 with Masters of Architecture as well as Landscape Architecture. For the next two months, she biked and camped her way across the North American Continent. Currently, she lives and practices landscape architecture in New York City. At the firm terrain-nyc, she works on projects that include the design of green roofs, water purification/ filtration gardens, rooftop terraces, low-technology water collection and dissemination techniques, and public courtyards.

SASHA RABIN
NATURAL BUILDING DESIGN CHARRETTE, BUILDING WITH COB, STRAWBALE AND MORE: NATURAL WALL SYSTEMS

Sasha has a degree in Ecological Design from Evergreen State College. She has studied natural and traditional methods of building in Mexico, Belize, Guatemala, Indonesia, and the southwest United States. Following an apprenticeship at the Cob Cottage Company, she worked with them as an assistant instructor and went on to co-found Seven Generation Natural Builders (SGNB; www.sgnb.com). She built a cob dwelling in the southwest U.S. where she currently resides. She continues to teach with SGNB, and a guest instructor at the Real Goods Institute for Solar Living and Yestermorrow Design/Build School.

JACOB DEVA RACUSIN
NATURAL BUILDING DESIGN CHARRETTE, BUILDING WITH COB, STRAWBALE AND MORE: NA-
TRAL WALL SYSTEMS, LIME PLASTERS, NATURAL PAINTS AND FINISHES, EARTHEN FLOORS

Jacob has been creating functional art with wood, stone, straw, earth, and other assorted materials since 2000, when he began design and construction on a solar-oriented straw bale house in Montgomery, Vermont, in which he lives with his family. Through contracting, consulting, teaching, and lots of tinkering, he explores particular interests in cold-climate straw bale construction, natural painting and plastering, bioregional design and construction, and the integration between buildings and their environments.

TIMOTHY RIETH
DIRECTOR, NATURAL BUILDING INTENSIVE PROGRAM; NATURAL BUILDING DESIGN CHARRETTE,
BUILDING WITH COB, STRAWBALE AND MORE: NATURAL WALL SYSTEMS, ROCKET STOVE, CLAY
PLASTERS, EARTHEN FLOORS

See editor biographies, page 123.

ABOUT
THE INTENSIVE STUDENTS

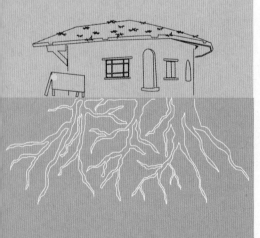

HOKE CAGLE

Hoke Cagle holds a B.A. in Natural Resources and Anthropology from Sewanee College, and has working interests in gross material processes and objective irony. Through his continuing explorations in ecology, culture, and education, Hoke believes that addressing issues of global warming and greater human happiness and harmony will lead to an increase in natural building, a greater embrace of the simple and beautiful life, and a more equitable world. Hoke is a blood native of the southern Appalachian Mountains.

DANA DAVIS

Dana grew up in rural Pennsylvania on her grandparent's farm. She teaches art in Philadelphia, but her agricultural childhood has inspired her to move from "The City that Loves You Back" to mountainous Vermont. Dana will apply the skills she developed in the Natural Building Intensive to the construction of her future timber frame/straw bale home.

DANA DAVIS

PAGE HOUSER

Page was born in San Antonio, Texas and received his B.F.A. from Texas State University, San Marcos and his M.F.A. from the Art Center College of Design in Pasadena, California. Upon graduating from the Art Center, he and his family moved to Brooklyn, New York to pursue their creative destinies. To support them, Page washed high-rise windows with his cousin and later established his own company. During this time they did the starving-artist-thing for 10 years in the Gotham City, and were facing schooling issues for three young kids. They moved back to Texas and the years rolled on. Page says, "It stuns me that my children are now teenagers, but now from this vantage point in my life I feel prepared to leverage my collected abilities, creative strengths, and entrepreneurial spirit to envision a meaningful and sustainable legacy."

The summer at Yestermorrow was personally transitional and pivotal for Page in numerous ways. "The Natural Building Intensive program was confirmation for me to integrate my previously-gained conventional building skills with the tried and true natural building methodologies that have served countless generations, cultures, communities. For me, green or natural building is not so much the creation of a structure but a focused means of creating communities that are responsive to the critical, local needs of the people that inhabit them."

JOSH KOPPEN

Josh grew up in Sheffield Lake, Ohio (almost Anytown, USA) and attended art school for a few years. When it seemed to be primarily an ego factory, he left for the West Coast and was introduced to earthships and the whole idea of sustainability. After these seeds were planted, Josh did some backpacking around the world and then returned to Ohio. He recalls, "All the while during my travels I was reading, doodling, and dreaming up ideas of homesteads and city parks that educate and entertain (edutain). After seven years of steeping in this stuff, I've found myself in the wonderfully fitting program at Yestermorrow, which probably saved me from a lifetime of waiting tables and idle daydreaming."

KEVIN MANLEY

Kevin started building skateboard ramps when he was about ten years old. The first one was awkwardly patched together and arguably a little unsafe, but the more he built, the better they got. Over the years while developing a love for skating (and all board sports for that matter), Kevin was also developing a love for building. However, building took a backseat for a while as interests in art, photography and illustration led Kevin to a professional career as a graphic designer in Atlanta. Design became his new passion, and he fully immersed himself in it for eight years after college. As much as design work satisfied him in certain respects, he began miss working with his hands; "I missed the craft of building," he says. "As I was making this realization, a friend loaned me the book Homework and I was so inspired by the featured lifestyles and homes that I dislodged myself from the professional world and took up the task of learning to design and build my own home. I am drawn to small structures and cabins and I still love working with wood, but what really gets me stoked is using less conventional materials like cob and straw bale."

115

JUAN JOSÉ MARTINEZ BRUN

"My name is Juan José Martinez Brun, and I live in Guadalajara, Mexico where I am a self-employed architect/builder. I consider myself a creative and sensitive person and like to take challenges. My passions include working with my hands creating art and handicrafts as well as a love for being outdoors especially in the mountains and forest where I feel a strong connection with trees. Additionally, I like to read, do yoga, and meditate. I find that natural building is a great tool for me to use my creativity in a hands-on way while helping people build their homes in a way that is in harmony with Mother Earth."

WILL McSWAIN

Will is a young builder and a seeker of the Way. After studying sociology and religious studies, he pursued carpentry, which taught him valuable skills, but the work left him feeling unsatisfied with the conventional building process. The desire to continue building and using his body led Will to Yestermorrow. He is presently excited to pursue natural building. He loves to look at the sky, get lost in music, and take walks in the dark. Will says he is "a constant dreamer of a world that is yet to be seen, a world that is a seed inside us all, and when it blooms the joy of springtime will resound forever."

JASON PRICE

JASON PRICE

Jason Price lives with his beautiful family in Cuttingsville, Vermont. After studying Land and Resource Management at Sterling College, Jason founded Sōl to Soul Seeds, which is committed to sustainable food production in the present and future. Jason is dedicated to bridging social and environmental gaps by learning and living holistically.

Yestermorrow is all about sustainability, from its recycled headquarters building that was once a popular inn, to its portable trailer's solar-electrical system.

YESTERMORROW
DESIGN/BUILD SCHOOL

Yestermorrow Design/Build School is a non-profit institution founded in 1980. The School currently offers more than 150 studio, shop, and hands-on courses that are taught by 111 faculty members. The School is nationally recognized for its teaching methods, attention to craftsmanship and innovation, and emphasis on sustainable and artful approaches to community, system, and building design.

THE MISSION

Yestermorrow Design/Build School inspires people to create a better, more sustainable world by providing hands-on education that integrates design and craft as a creative, interactive process.

THE PHILOSOPHY

Yestermorrow's courses are specifically designed to demystify the designing and building processes using hands-on, experiential learning to teach students the art and wisdom of good design and the skill and savvy of enduring craftsmanship as a single, integrated process.

This creative process offers students unique insight into the oftentimes disparate worlds of the architect and the builder. Architects are routinely trained without any building experience that might inform their designs, and builders are trained to execute without a sense of the overarching purpose or design of the project.

Combining design and building offers numerous advantages and promotes the creation of intentional and inspired buildings and communities that

Nature and designing with nature are big parts of Yestermorrow's campus and curriculum. The pond is often home to local beavers and a resident great blue heron.

Yestermorrow is also home to one of the nation's first wheelchair accessible tree houses. Good design and beauty should be available to all.

enhance our world. From the professional design/builder to the do-it-yourself design/build homeowner, every designer should know how to build and every builder should know how to design. This philosophy sets Yestermorrow apart from other educational institutions.

FOR MORE INFORMATION about the School, visit www.yestermorrow.org.

Yestermorrow offers quality classes for all skill levels, ages and backgrounds.

ABOUT
THE EDITORS

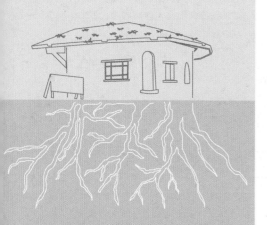

Tim became a builder by a somewhat unorthodox route beginning with his professional career as an archaeologist. Living and working in villages on small islands in the Pacific, which have rich histories of indigenous, vernacular architectural traditions, led him to question the ubiquity of concrete block and corrugated metal houses in the tropics and the equally puzzling OSB and vinyl-sided homes in temperate climes. These ponderings led to training and collaboration with some of the pioneers in North America's natural building movement including Ianto Evans, Linda Smiley, and Athena and Bill Steen. Tim eventually co-founded Seven Generations Natural Builders, an education and consultation collective that specializes in earth and straw construction. Tim continues to participate in archaeological research in the Pacific, with ongoing projects in Hawai'i, Fiji, Samoa, and Palau. He is a long-distance runner, haphazard gardener, and member of the FVK-SF (Fearless Vampire Killers, Order of Saint Francis).

TIMOTHY RIETH

Bob's professional journey has taken him from wildlife conservation and habitat restoration to making seminal contributions in the fields of environmental quality and sustainability. During his pre-Yestermorrow days, Bob helped restore the gray wolf to Yellowstone National Park and oyster bars to the Chesapeake Bay. He championed the cause of family farmers and pushed for conservation practices on agricultural lands. And, more recently, he launched the Fossil Free by '33 movement in Southern California. He is an accomplished writer, educator, and strategic thinker who has held senior positions with the Wildlife Habitat Council, Defenders of Wildlife, the Chesapeake Bay Foundation and the Community Environmental Council. He has served on numerous boards and advisory panels dealing with thorny issues ranging from alien invasive species control and sewage abatement to freeway widening and airport redesign. Bob's current interests include green building, urban redevelopment, transportation planning, relocalization, renewable energy, and water systems. Bob lives in Warren, VT where he hikes, kayaks, fishes, paints, and writes bad poetry in his spare time. He is learning to love winter with his wife, Carlene Marie Ramus, a green architect and landscape designer.

BOB FERRIS

The door is always open at the folly.

READINGLIST

Alexander, Christopher, Sara Ishikawa, and Murray Silverstein with Max Jacobson, Igrid Fiksdahl-King and Shlomo Angel. *A Pattern Language.* New York: Oxford University Press, 1977.

Alexander, C. *The Timeless Way of Building.* New York: Oxford University Press, 1979.

Beemer, Will. "Introduction to Scribing I" *Timber Framing # 76*, June 2005, pp. 4-13. Becket, MA: Journal of the Timber Framers Guild.

Beemer, Will. "Introduction to Scribing II" *Timber Framing # 77*, September 2005, pp. 4-9. Becket, MA: Journal of the Timber Framers Guild.

Beemer, Will. "Introduction to Scribing III" *Timber Framing # 78*, December 2005, pp. 18-22. Becket, MA: Journal of the Timber Framers Guild.

Chambers, Robert Wood. *The Log Construction Manual: The Ultimate Guide to Building Handcrafted Log Homes.* White River Junction, VT: Deep Stream Press dist. By Chelsea Green, 2006.

Connell, John B. *Homing Instinct.* New York, New York: Warner Books. 1993.

Earth Pledge and William McDonough. *Green Roofs: Ecological Design and Construction.* Atglen, PA: Schiffer Publishing, 2005.

Evans, Ianto, Michael G. Smith, and Linda Smiley. *The Hand-Sculpted House.* White River Junction, Vermont: Chelsea Green, 2002.

Houben, Hugo and Hubert Guillard. *Earth Construction: A Comprehensive Guide.* London: Intermediate Technology Publications, 1994.

Holmes, Stafford and Michael Wingate. *Building with Lime: A Practical Guide.* Bourton-on-Dunsmore, Rugby, Warwickshire, United Kingdom: ITDG (Practical Action Publishing), 2002.

Kennedy, Joseph F., Michael G. Smith, and Catherine Wanek (eds). *The Art of Natural Building.* Gabriola Island, British Columbia: New Society Publishers, 2002. Holmes, Stafford and Michael Wingate. *Building with Lime: A Practical Guide.* Bourton-on-Dunsmore, Rugby, Warwickshire, United Kingdom: ITDG (Practical Action Publishing), 2002.

Khalili, Nader. *Ceramic Houses and Earth Architecture.* San Francisco: Burning Gate Press, 1990.

King, Bruce. *Buildings of Earth and Straw.* Sausalito, CA: Ecological Design Press, 1996.

King, Bruce. *Design of Straw Bale Buildings.* San Rafael, California: Green Building Press, 2006.

Lacinski, Paul and Michael Bergeron. *Serious Straw Bale: A Construction Guide for All Climates.* White River Junction, Vermont: Chelsea Green, 2000.

Lawless, Julia and Lynn Edwards. *The Natural Paint Book.* New York: Rodale Press, 2003.

Magwood, Chris, Peter Mack, and Tina Therrien. *More Straw Bale Building: A Complete Guide to Designing and Building with Straw.* Gabriola Island, British Columbia, Canada: New Society Publishers, 2005.

McHenry, Jr, Paul Graham. Adobe and Rammed Earth Buildings. Tucson: University of Arizona Press, 1989.

Smith, M.G. "Foundations for Natural Buildings" in *The Art of Natural Building.* Joseph F. Kennedy. Gabriola Island, BC, Canada: New Society Publishers, 2002.

Snodgrass, Edmund C. and Lucie L. Snodgrass. *Green Roof Plants.* Portland, OR: Timber Press, 2006.

Steen, Athena, Bill Steen, and David Bainbridge (with David Eisenberg). *The Straw Bale House.* White River Junction, Vermont: Chelsea Green, 1994.

Steen, Athena and Bill Steen. *Earthen Floors.* Elgin, AZ, Canelo Project, 1996.

Steen, Athena and Bill Steen. "Earthen Floors" in *The Art of Natural Building.* Joseph F. Kennedy, Michael G. Smith, and Catherine Wanek (eds). Gabriola Island, British Columbia: New Society Publishers, 2002.

Tom, R., "Rubble Trench Foundations" in *The Art of Natural Building.* Joseph F. Kennedy. Gabriola Island, BC, Canada: New Society Publishers, 2002.

Vivian, John. *Building Stone Walls.* North Adams, Massachusetts: Storey Publishing, 1976.

Weismann, Adam and Katy Bryce. *Building with Cob.* Foxhole, Dartington, Totnes, Devon: Green Books Ltd, 2006.

MORE RESOURCES can be found online at www.yestermorrow.org/links.html.

WWW.YESTERMORROW.ORG